THIS BOOK IS FOR

BORN

LOTS OF LOVE
FORVER & ALWAYS

Made in the USA
Las Vegas, NV
06 May 2022

48482797R00085